St Mary's Day

The Story of a Seaside Village
&
The Lost Fishing Fleets of
Dymchurch & Littlestone

by

Vic Haisell

Published by
Hythe Bookshop
86 High Street, Hythe, Kent

British Library cataloguing in publication data
A catalogue record of this book is available
from the British Library

Printed in Great Britain by
Principal Colour
Principal House, Hop Pocket Lane
Paddock Wood Kent TN12 6DQ

ISBN 0 9544331 0 6

Contents

Acknowledgements

Most of the photographs are from my own collection, but I would like to express my appreciation to the following for the loan of their photographs. Derek Apps, The Barnes family, Ted Carey, Dennis Cole, Jean Edmonds, June Finn, Sid Goodsell, Freddy Harridine, Gena Rouse and Dave Wood.

I would also like to offer my thanks to June Finn for writing the foreword, to Andy Crawford and Steve Wakerell for producing the electronic draft and to Chris Lock for reading and amending the final manuscript.

Foreword

As hamlets and villages all over the country grow out of recognition, it is good to think that someone who was born, has grown up and lived his life in the area, is willing to put pen to paper and make a record of what, at first glance might have appeared to be an insignificant hamlet that has grown into a large village.

As with his first book of childhood wartime memories, *Wartime St Mary's Bay* Vic has put a lot of time into preparing this book cajoling friends and relatives for photographs and tapping their memories to add to his vast knowledge of the area.

The book covers subjects of, I think great interest, from the change of name from Jesson to St Mary's Bay, the Coastguard Station, the Lifeboat, the Royal Flying Corps (subsequently the Royal Air Force), the camp that housed them which became the famous children's holiday camp, the airfield, the Boys' Brigade annual visits and all the other things that made this a really self contained hamlet with no need to travel to shop outside the area.

Towards the end of the book Vic has also written about the local sea fishing industry which was and still is one of the activities most dear to his heart. Both fishing and shrimping are hard work, jobs he still enjoys. In the last three or four decades it was, at times sad to see the close-knit community being overwhelmed by new estates and buildings, but it is all adding new elements to our area's history.

It has given me much pleasure to write these few words for Vic's new book and I sincerely hope you will enjoy reading it as much as I have.

June (Beale) Finn

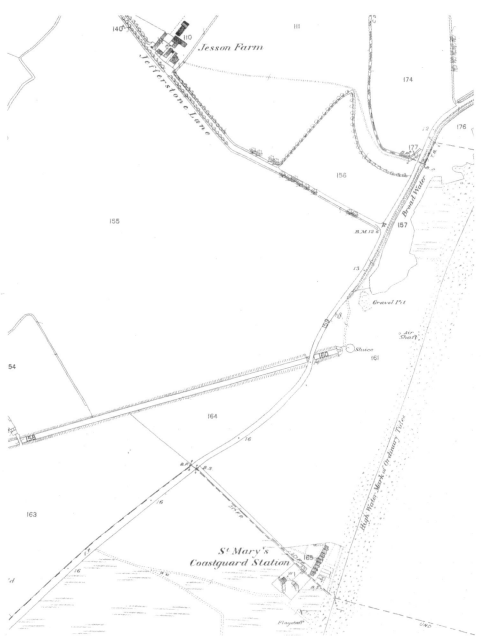

A map drawn in 1863 showing from the top, Jesson Farm, just below centre the New Cut sewer and out-fall, and at the bottom St Mary's Coast Guard Station with its outbuildings, green and flagstaff. Most of this site was claimed by the sea in the early 1900s. The future A259, at this time a simple cart track can be seen winding its way along the coast. A new road further to the north of the present A259 which was proposed in the 1930s was never built.

St Mary's Bay 1800 – 1975

Origins

The origins of the village we now know as St Mary's Bay date from the early days of the nineteenth century. Prior to that time there was very little evidence of human habitation along the stretch of coast where the village now stands. A traveller making his way along the winding road from Dymchurch to New Romney would have seen on his left the English Channel and a wide arc of unblemished shoreline fading into the distance of Dungeness. On the landward side the village of St Mary in the Marsh would have been marked by the low steeple of the church of St Mary the Virgin. A few distant farmsteads might have been visible but close to the shore the only signs of human presence would have been the sheepfolds and looker's huts – the shelters used by shepherds during lambing time – dotted here and there on the broad sheep pastures.

In 1804, the threat of invasion by the forces of Napoleon, which had existed for some years prompted the decision to construct a line of defence in the shape of the Royal Military Canal and a chain of Martello Towers running from Aldeburgh in Suffolk to Seaford in Sussex. Two of these towers, numbered 26 and 27 were the first brick-built structures to appear on the St Mary's Bay shoreline. Tower No 26 was built on the eastern side of the Gobsden Gut (now Cobsden Sewer), an outfall which ran into the sea near the present Dunstall Lane. Tower No 27 was built approximately a quarter of a mile to the west. Neither tower stands today. Damaged by sea erosion, No 27 was demolished in 1841and the other tower lasted until 1871. The site of Tower 26 was on what is now the sea wall next to the car park opposite Dunstall Lane – roughly in front of where the toilet block now stands. Its partner was further along the car park towards St Mary's Bay – approximately opposite the fish and chip shop (formerly the Cobsden Cafe).

My own impression of the 1830 Martello Towers 26 and 27 near the cart track that later became the main A259. The towers are standing on either side of the Cobsden sewer (Gobsden Gut). In the distance stands the row of Blockade cottages at the St Mary's Coastguard Station

After demolition of the towers both sites remained in the hands of the War Department until the late 1920s when they were sold for about £50. A short time later they were resold to the Lords of the Level of Romney Marsh and incorporated into what became High Knock car park. At one time there were stones marking the sites but they have since been buried. Wraight Brothers, the Dymchurch builders used to pay the Level £5 a year to mow and have the hay off the land.

The Coast Blockade

Smuggling was rampant all around the coast, particularly in this area and in the early 1800s, a force, known as the Coast Blockade was formed in an attempt to combat the problem.

The force was made up of naval personnel. Sailors who were used to spending their working lives at sea now found themselves based ashore. Many were drawn from the lowest ranks, the 'waisters' who carried out the most menial tasks below decks. In their new working environment the men were knocked into shape by the strictest discipline, a well known dispenser of which was Captain William McCulloch RN, an officer widely known as 'Flogging Joey'.

Blockade personnel practising semaphore on top of a Martello Tower.

In the 1820s a Blockade Station, known as the St Mary's Coastguard Station was built. Located near the high tide line, its site was on the sea side of the present Rugby Club chalets. There were nine single storey cottages facing the sea, in the centre one of which lived the Chief Boatman.

The nearby parade ground, a large green with flagstaff was where the men would assemble before marching to their headquarters at Tower 27.

The tower provided an excellent lookout and vantage point from which to signal by semaphore with other stations and shipping in the Channel. It was at this tower that the first lifeboat used in the East Bay (Hythe Bay) was stationed, having been introduced at the suggestion of Captain McCulloch. The tower was close to the East Road Shipping Lane and weather-bound vessels, unable to proceed down the Channel would anchor in the lea of the land on the Hythe side of Dungeness Point. Many found themselves in trouble when their anchors dragged or were lost and sudden changes in wind direction made vessels vulnerable to running aground.

The Lifeboat

Based at Tower 27, the first lifeboat was built by William Plenty and owned by the RNLI. The station was known as Dymchurch No 27 Tower and the crew were all members of the Coast Blockade. It was several years before Dungeness, Littlestone and Hythe received their first lifeboats.

On 27th August 1832, the lifeboat was launched in a full gale to aid the vessel *Osiris* floundering between Littlestone and Tower 27. The lifeboat crew managed to rescue all the men aboard the ship. For this remarkable feat the coxswain F.S. Henshaw received the RNLI Silver Medal.

On 1st October 1835 the brig *Industry* washed down the bay completely out of control dragging her anchor in gale force conditions. All the crew were saved by the gallant men from the Dymchurch Station. The Chief Boatman, Lt. John Summerville RN, received the Gold Medal for his courage and leadership. What a great achievement! The lifeboat service does not give away medals easily.

The lifeboat was again in service on 13th October 1835 when it was badly damaged attempting to assist a pilot cutter caught in a full gale with heavy rain and sleet. A replacement vessel, designed and built by Paxton came into service on 3rd December 1836. Within a fortnight, on 16th December she was called into service in very bad weather to assist a collier aground on the Newcome Bar. Eleven men were saved before the vessel began to break up.

A few weeks later another small ship drifted onto the same sand bar. After standing by for four hours in very heavy swell, the lifeboat was able to come alongside. Despite being seriously damaged in a collision with the stricken ship the lifeboat managed to rescue the crew and return to the station.

After being sent away for repair she never returned. Instead she was sold to the other side of the world to serve as a coastal lifeboat in Australia. This signalled the end of the Dymchurch lifeboat station.

The Coastguards continued at Tower 27 for another three years. In 1840 the sea, which had long been threatening began to take control. The decision was made to demolish the tower and in the following year it was pulled down.

With the tower gone the Coastguard continued to work from home at the St Mary's Station. One duty was to help man the Littlestone lifeboat when they were short of crew. One occasion when this happened was on 6th March 1891 when two coastguards and a Chief Boatman were summoned to make up the crew of the *Sandal Magna*. Two schooners, *The Echo* and the *High Barley* of Fleetwood were caught in an easterly gale with heavy snow showers. It was some of the worst weather ever recorded along the coast and the ships were in serious danger.

After three failed attempts to get the lifeboat afloat the crew finally managed to get her away. The vessel immediately overturned throwing a man into the boiling sea. No sooner had the lifeboat been righted and the crewman hauled aboard when she capsized again. Coastguard William Ryan was swept out of sight and lost.

When the boat overturned for a third time all hands were thrown into the sea. All but two managed to wash ashore, some within three-quarters of a mile of

The headstone of the Chief Boatman Thomas Sullivan who drowned on the 9th March 1891 while serving on the Littlestone lifeboat. Also the grave of Samuel Hart, Boatman. With it is the name of William Ryan whose body was never found. All from the St Mary's Station.

the lifeboat house, others as far along the coast as Romney Hoy, quite close to where the greens and beach huts are to be found at Littlestone.

The launchers back at the boathouse were unaware of what had happened, thinking that the lifeboat was still on course for the schooners. Later they were to discover the truth that the three coastguards – all from the St Mary's Station – had been drowned.

The Chief Boatman Thomas Sullivan and his Colleague Samuel Hart were buried with full ceremonial honours in New Romney churchyard. This was also the last resting place of four victims from the schooners. The body of William Ryan was never recovered.

This must have been a very traumatic experience for the families and colleagues of the lifeboatmen back at the coastguard station at St Mary's, miles from anywhere.

Many years later a workman cleaning out a dyke at Dymchurch found a brass memorial plate commemorating the gallantry of the men who lost their lives on this rescue. Another coastguard who was in the boat on that shout and survived the ordeal was Mr James Furber who lived in Littlestone until he was over 100 years old. I remember him around Littlestone when I was going to school in New Romney.

On a lighter note, it appears the coastguard station was provided with a donkey for carrying supplies and water. Apparently they were standard issue for remote stations. One animal was so bad tempered they wanted to get rid of him and in 1839 the following order was issued:

"The board having ordered the disposal of the donkey at No 27 Tower, I have to direct, in the first place, that the one now at that station be exchanged for one at Lydd Station, as complaints of the latter have been made to me of his being of vicious habits. As soon as this takes place, the commanding Boatman of 27 Tower will sell the donkey of Dymchurch by Public Auction."

The Loss of the Station

In 1887 the first groynes or breakwaters were constructed to counteract erosion by the sea. Even in those days the high water mark had begun to rise.

The precaution was to no avail as the sea first claimed the green, complete with flagstaff and then the cottages. This left only a few outbuildings and one cottage which had no connection with the coastguard station. These buildings were on the land that was later to be purchased and built on by Rugby School. The cottage which stood near the sea wall was demolished in the late 1940s. According to local people it had been owned by a Russian gentleman and was known generally as the 'Russian House'.

On the Dymchurch side of Jesson was Cobden Bungalow built in 1900 by William Body of Tenterden. In those days the Body family owned a considerable amount of land around the area.

I remember in the late 1940s when we had had a gale of wind from the north the ground swell would expose what the locals called the 'fret'. This was the very fine grit, usually black, which was under the main beach. I would go with my father and look for coins and rings that had been lost by holiday makers in the summer. Sometimes we would find quite a lot of money – shillings, sixpences, lots of pennies, a few half crowns and occasionally a decent ring. This occupation was known locally as 'fretting'.

I had the job of cleaning the tarnished coins by first soaking them in vinegar and then scouring them with a wire brush. If you were given a dirty coin in your change in a shop or a pub it was known as a 'fretter'. When we were fretting over by the Rugby Club's Camp we would often find bricks that had washed out of the sand. These, my father told me, had come from the old coastguard station.

The Hamlet of Jesson

Apart from the coast road, the main thoroughfare through St Mary's Bay is Jefferstone Lane from which Jesson, the name of the original hamlet derives.

Jesson Farm, which was built around 1820 consisted of two houses, which are still standing and a number of outbuildings. These were close to the Light Railway and were eventually demolished to make way for housing development. Some years after the farm was built, a pair of semi-detached farmworkers' cottages were erected further down the lane. My mother's father, Seaman Beale and his wife moved into one of them in 1878 after getting married in St Mary's Church. The cottages were later converted into one house named Jesson Cottage and became the home of William Apps. Known locally as 'Mopper', a nickname he totally disliked, Apps worked all his life on the Marsh as a much respected looker (shepherd). A large field beside the cottage which Apps made into a camping site later became Jesson Court Caravan Park.

ROMNEY MARSHES FROM HOLIDAY CAMP.

William 'Mopper' Apps' house in Jesson Lane showing the large field which was later to become the site of Jesson Court Caravan Park

As a schoolboy I used to walk past Jesson Cottage after being dropped by the bus at the top of the Lane. Sometimes Mr Apps would be sitting by his garden fence and I would love to stop and talk to him. He always had something interesting to say about the old days on the Marsh and I wish I could remember everything he told me.

One day he invited me to go eel fishing with him. Over many years of fishing he had covered most of the sewers on Romney Marsh. The venue on this occasion was the New Cut, the main sewer that enters the sea in St Mary's Bay.

A net with corks arranged along the top and lead weights attached to the lower line was set across the sewer from bank to bank. Part of the net formed a long sock or tail into which the eels would swim and be trapped. Two men looked after the net, one on each bank. Back up the sewer a rope with a length of heavy chain attached to it was stretched over the water by two other men. Working towards the net, the men raised the rope high into the air

'Mopper' and Mrs Apps at the rear of their house. Both are wearing their 'Sunday best' and are perhaps preparing to leave for church.

before letting it drop into the murky water, stirring up the mud and disturbing the eels. When the men on the rope reached the net, the net was retrieved and the catch sorted out. As well as eels there were small bass, mullet and mud butts (flounders). After the eels were gathered up into a sack the net was set further up the cut and the operation repeated.

While all this was happening 'Mopper', who was getting on in years followed us in a kind of hand-pedalled wheelchair, bellowing out orders and waving his walking stick in the air. What a character he was – they don't make them like that anymore!

The Airfield

The development of Jesson did not begin in earnest until the 1914-18 War when the War Department built a camp. This was to house the Royal Flying Corps No1 (Auxiliary) School of Gunnery amalgamated with No 1 (Observers) School of Aerial Gunnery.

The camp was intended to accommodate 1000 men, 300 NCOs, 400 officers and 400 women. It was estimated that from each intake 400 trained pilots would receive their wings.

Initially they used a landing strip on Romney Warren and part of the Littlestone Golf Course but soon moved to a proper aerodrome in Jesson Lane. This occupied 75 acres of land bounded by Jesson Lane and the Jefferstone and Cobsden Sewers.

Administration and living quarters were located on the western side of Jesson Lane close to where it meets the main coast road. The field on the Dymchurch side was used to build sheds for transport and engineering. The main transport garages were close to the main road and were used for servicing large lorries and planes. In later years the end of the building facing into Jesson Lane was converted to a shop and became Jesson Post Office.

Further down the lane on the eastern side was the carpenters' shop. With most of the aircraft being built with wooden frames the carpenters' skills were much in demand. Tears and holes in the aircrafts' linen-covered fuselages and wings were repaired in the adjacent sailmakers' shop. In the adjoining dope shop shellac was applied to stiffen up and waterproof the linen, giving it great strength. The planes were then ready to return to service.

One of the airfield workshops later became Marshland Bakery owned by Ray Smith of Dymchurch. In its heyday during the three decades after the Second World War the bakery was an important local employer. There were shops in Dymchurch, New Romney and Greatstone as well as in St Mary's Bay itself. As many as seven vans delivered door to door all over the Marsh and two bakers worked all night to meet the demand. Special large loaves were baked for the children's holiday camp.

Littlestone (Jesson) Airfield

Airfields were often square-shaped to enable take off and landing in any direction. Planes in those days had to take off and land directly into the wind. The chalk circle identified the airfield and provided an aid to direction. Harold Whitehead who lived at Jesson Farm (just behind the trees in the bottom left corner) maintained the chalk circle and ensured that the field was kept clear of livestock when aircraft were landing or taking off.

The camp power station is just to the right of the RH&DR platform shelter. 'Mopper' Apps' house stands to the left of Jesson Lane which winds its way through the trees and past a group of bungalows. These were a self-build project in which local building workers including Dan Apps, Ted Best and Bill Finn participated. The site of the present sports field is on the other side of the lane. The Jesson Club is just visible in the extreme bottom left corner.

RFC Pilot standing by his BE.2e at Littlestone (Jesson) Aerodrome. Behind the aircraft is one of the Bessoneau Hangars. Made from canvas and fitted to a wooden frame, they were held down by screw-type pegs secured in concrete weights. There were about fifteen such hangars set around the airfield. The BE.2e was one of the first British-designed military aircraft by B.E. Bleriot Experimental (no connection with Louis Bleriot) designed by Geoffrey de Havilland and F.M. Green at the Royal Aircraft Factory in 1911. The one shown would probably have had a larger 90hp Renault engine fitted, with a maximum speed of 90 mph and a service ceiling of about 10,000 feet. On service over the Western Front in France they suffered very heavy losses in combat with German Fockers and were withdrawn.

Westland WAPITI 2a. Built for the Royal Air Force by Westland Aircraft Company at Yeovil in Somerset. This plane served with No 604 (County of Middlesex) Auxiliary Squadon and visted Jesson (Littlestone) Aerodrome in 1930. The following year the aircraft crashed at Tangmere and was a write-off.

An illuminated wind direction arrow in the corner of the field nearest Dymchurch. A smaller one was in the opposite corner near the bridge in Jesson Lane.

Lt Chapman's bits and pieces aeroplane. He also used an airstrip at Warren Road, Littlestone. Leaving Jesson, he would fly to Warren Road, taking a windsock with him. He would set this up and take people up for paying flights. Afterwards the sock would come down and he would fly back to Jesson.

There are only a few of these buildings still standing, one being the coal yard which was owned by Cyril Jenner, a local councillor and coal merchant for many years.

While the Flying Corps were here Jesson Farm was used as offices and the large barn as a cinema and theatre complete with a stage. The highlight of passing out was a party and concert held in the barn.

Near the flying field and where the Light Railway line now runs stand four long brick-built sheds. Two of them were used for photographic laboratories and dark rooms. All the film taken by the air crews of the mock dog fights, aerial gunnery and target practice were processed there. Edith Nesbit, the author owned two sheds that were later turned into bungalows. In fact she lived there for some two years and most of the time was in ill health. Her husband Captain Tucker named the bungalows Longboat and Jollyboat. Both still stand today and can be seen at the bottom of Nesbit Road.

The last building belonging to the Flying Corps' camp was the power station on the right of Jesson Lane just past the Light Railway station. This brick building housed two large single cylinder paraffin engines with enormous flywheels. The engines were started by using blowlamps and would generate enough electricity to meet the demands of the camp as well as some of the properties nearby. After the 1st World War the engineer in charge was Mr Charles Colmer who later started his own electrical business and used one room at the end of this bungalow as a shop. Graham Foord now owns the business.

The Guard Room was at the top of Jefferstone Lane in the corner on the left opposite the transport garages. All the camp accommodation was on this side of the road. The first building block was the officers' mess and dining hall. The black hut was the station HQ and was later to become Charles Colmer's electrical shop.

Jesson Farm showing the two barns. The one nearest the farmhouse was used as a cinema and theatre during the the Royal Flying Corps days. The dairy is painted white on the end facing into Jesson Lane and was used as a shop selling eggs, milk and home made ice-cream.

The third group of buildings were the airmen's billets, cookhouse and a hospital. After the war Lt Chapman was left in charge of the camp with a care and maintenance party. He lived in and later purchased the hospital. He built a plane out of parts that had been left by the Flying Corps and flew it regularly. After his death his wife lived on for many years and was a very good friend of my mother.

The last building near the railway line was the mortuary. With a lot of student pilots flying and practising combat manoeuvres and dog fights,

The Camp. The top narrow field with the hedge is Mr Apps' Camping Site. The very small building in the top right corner is the mortuary. The Light Railway runs across the photograph just behind the mortuary. In front and to the left of the mortuary are the Liverpool Hall and kitchens. To the left of these are the dormitories of the Lancashire complex. The dark building in the centre foreground is Mr Colmer's (now Graham Foord's) electrical shop. Lt Chapman's bungalow is the white building behind Colmer's. The building with the white roof to the right of Jesson Lane is the Marshland Bakery.

casualties must have been quite high. When the airforce left and the aerodrome became a holiday camp the mortuary was used as a meat store.

After the armistice in 1919, when the School for Aerial Gunnery was moved to Manston, the flying field was kept open to provide emergency landing facilities for the newly-established civil air services flying from Croydon to Paris and Brussels.

Although Lympne was the south coast customs airport it was particularly susceptible to fog. On occasions when fog enveloped Lympne planes were diverted to Littlestone (Jesson). The airfield was known as the Littlestone Emergency Landing Ground probably because the first airstrip was on part of the Littlestone golf links.

In the centre of the field was a large white circle made from blocks of whitewashed chalk. The name Littlestone was painted across the centre of the circle. Set at intervals around the circumference were tallish beacons, which at night constantly blinked and showed a red light. They were operated by gas and serviced by the ground crews from Lympne. When planes landed taxis would arrive to collect the passengers and their luggage and take them on to their destinations or another airfield.

When in 1925 the Romney, Hythe and Dymchurch railway was laid it cut across the top of the aerodrome leaving a rectangular flying field.

During the late twenties and the thirties the field was the venue of some spectacular air displays. One famous airman was Sir Alan Cobham with his flying circus. His team performed wing walking, parachuting and dare devil low flying. On some weekends in the summer it was possible for the public to take pleasure flights. On one occasion my mother took one and thoroughly enjoyed it, especially the view from the air of the Marsh and its surrounding area.

As air travel became more reliable with larger aircraft being used demand for the emergency landing facilities at Littlestone diminished. Just before the Second World War the landing lights were switched off for the last time and removed. The land reverted back to farmland and has remained so to this day.

The Development of the Holiday Camp

A few years before the First World War the London Boys' Brigade held summer camps under canvas on William Body's land behind Cobsden, just off Dunstall Lane. When the Royal Flying Corps' Gunnery School was up for sale in 1920 the Boy's Brigade purchased all the accommodation on the New Romney side of Jesson Lane excluding the homes of Mr Colmer and Lt Chapman.

After a year or two, finding it difficult to maintain they sold it to Allnett's, a northern building and development company. Captain Allnett started what became the Dymchurch Holiday Camp using most of the airforce buildings.

At about this time the Duke of York, later King George VI, had accepted the presidency of the Industrial Welfare Society. He conceived the experiment, which became famous as the Duke of York's Camp. This brought boys of different social status together annually to spend a holiday together by the sea. One hundred public schools and one hundred industrial concerns were each asked to send two boys to the camp, which was held at Jesson. Later the Duke of York's Camp was held at Southwold in Suffolk.

The Camp flourished in the late twenties and thirties. During this period three dining halls and kitchens were in use, and all the dormitories would be fully occupied by the children and their accompanying teachers.

In the mid 30s plans were drawn up for the construction of All Saints Church. Thus the hamlet of Jesson became the village of St Mary's Bay and in 1936 the name of the camp was changed.

In those days the camp was the biggest employer in the area during the summer and also kept a good gang of workmen to carry out maintenance during the closed season.

In World War Two, a number of the buildings were bombed, mainly those running alongside the A259. The Berkshire and Lancashire Kitchens never opened up after the war, all the catering being done in the Yorkshire Block in the centre of the camp.

The Boys' Brigade arriving at the holiday camp in 1929. The photo was taken in Jesson Lane close to the site of Graham Foord's electrical shop. The buses belonged to Carey Bros of New Romney.

The dining hall was known as York Hall and a large, adjoining kitchen was modernised to cope with all the cooking needs. Some of the Lancashire Block was never used again as accommodation although some new dormitories were built after the old one was demolished.

In the post-war years of the forties, fifties and early sixties the camp thrived with fleets of coaches packed with children and their teachers arriving on changeover day.

Part of the camp was taken over by Middlesex Schools who came every year bringing children from all over the county. The north was also well represented with many boys and girls from Manchester and Liverpool. When the Liverpool kids were here it did not matter whether you were over by the sea wall, down Jesson Lane or in the local shops, all you could hear was their distinct 'scouse' accent. It must have been great for them to come down to the seaside to breathe all that fresh air and explore the wide-open spaces of the Marsh.

During the season, the Boys' Brigade would arrive from London at New Romney Railway Station and march to the Camp headed by their band. On some Sundays they would also march down Jesson Lane to the Church of St Mary's in the Marsh for the morning service. On still days we used to remark how good the band sounded.

St Mary's Bay also had plenty of family holidaymakers who rented bungalows or stayed at other places such as the Sands Hotel, Golden Sands Holiday Camp and Apps' Caravan Site. Along the seawall there were several tea and ice cream kiosks and you could hire deck chairs from a Mrs Messiahs who with her husband had a large hut on the sea wall stacked full of chairs. On a fine day, the hut would be empty.

On the sands when the tide was out there were pony rides for children and every week a Punch and Judy show near the Sands Hotel. The Punch and Judy man rode a bicycle with a small trailer in which he carried his props. I think he came from Sellindge.

This was the golden era of the traditional British seaside holiday. With the advent of cheap air travel and the guarantee of Spanish sunshine, demand for this type of holiday waned and the local traders had to rely on day-trippers when the weather was fine.

During the Bank Holidays the Rugby Club would be down. I got to know a few of them – 'Saymos', 'Kilroy', 'Whip' (he would hold the money in the pub) and a character called 'Treacle'. I remember one day I was in the fisherman's hut on the Rugby Club sorting out some gear, when I was startled by two loud bangs. I looked out the door only to see Treacle standing there with a twelve bore shotgun under his arm. Both barrels were smoking and he was grinning.

"What's going on", I said. "I thought you had shot me".

He replied, "I was just taking a pop at a rabbit".

I said "You silly old bugger!".

Several former Rugby boys moved into the village. Ernie Benham and his brother Fred with their wives lived near the top of Jesson Lane. Ernie and

Turkeys being weighed and packed at St Mary's Bay Holiday Camp for Romney Marsh Poultry Ltd. Mrs F Apps is holding the pen and Mrs Simmons is to her right.

Fred were always over the beach fishing and bait digging. What a great couple of blokes they were.

Another Rugby member was Pat Barry. At the time he was the caretaker and lived in the Rugby Cottage. Later he and his wife moved to the Newlands Estate in Taylor's Lane. I will always remember Pat and his friends. On Boxing Day, whatever the weather they would take a dip in the sea. Pat also took a great interest in village affairs and became Chairman of the Council, a post he held for many years.

When the children's side of the holiday camp was scaled down, the name was changed again and it became known as the St Mary's Bay School Journey Centre. Most of the buildings down from the Light Railway were taken over by Romney Marsh Poultry who were still part of the same company that owned the Camp.

Turkey rearing became more intense and a hatchery was built in one of the former dormitories. After incubation and hatching, the chicks were put in

This very early photo of the camp looking towards the sea shows the canteen. The Sands Hotel is visible behind the trees. The dormitories Windsor and Newbury are on the right and the gate is close to where the new Village Hall car park entrance is today. I can remember several large bomb craters in this area during the war. A tank trap was dug across the sports ground to stop any German vehicles when an invasion was thought imminent in 1940.

pens and sheds near the railway line. When ready for the market the turkeys were killed and plucked and prepared for the table in one of the old dining halls. The period just before Christmas was always a busy time and many local people, especially women helped with the plucking. So much a bird – piecework!

In the 1970s the bulldozers moved in and demolition of the camp began. Starting near the Light Railway line the machines worked their way up to the main road. By the middle of the decade the first roads had been laid and William Bray started to build the bungalows along what is now Laurel Avenue. This was the start of the Tree Estate, as we know it today.

The Dymchurch Holiday Camp canteen was at the top of Jesson Lane and was built originally as the Guard Room for the Royal Flying Corps. It became the camp canteen where children could buy sweets and bottles of mineral water and was later renamed the camp Tuck Shop. It sold everything from buckets and spades to post cards. It was also the local Post Office.

Later, a newsagents, tobacconist and ice cream parlour was added and used by local people as well as holidaymakers. I remember a very pleasant lady Mrs Nellie Kerr worked there for many years. When St Mary's Post Office closed, the tuck shop again took over until it also became a victim of the bulldozer in the 1970s.

Jesson Lane. A view from the main road taken in the 1920s. Just visible on the extreme right is the end of one of the transport garages which was later St Mary's Bay Post Office. The next building was an ex-army hut named the Bungalow and owned for many years by Mr and Mrs Ernie Benham who first came here with the Rugby Club many years ago. In the black cottage next door lived Mr Kitchen who worked in the camp tuck shop. The large white building was originally part of the aerodrome and is still standing today. It was turned into a cottage called Sea Up and was the home of Mr and Mrs Joe Crisp. The next one with the three windows was called Teelin. On the opposite side of the lane and painted white is the camp hospital where Lt Chapman and his wife lived after the airfield closed.

The Dymchurch Holiday Camp. When the village of Jesson became known as St Mary's Bay in 1936 the camp also changed its name. This photo shows part of the Berkshire Block and the main road, which was very narrow in those days. It was near this spot that young Bernard Jenner was knocked down and killed in the 1930s by a car driven by the vicar of Faversham. The accident was a high talking point with the locals. "Book now for the 1931 season" is painted on the end of the building; on the other end "The largest holiday camp in England for boys and girls". This part of the camp housed the main offices. After the war the pink colour scheme was changed to cream, with blue woodwork and windows. In the 1940s the roofs of these buildings were blown off by a string of bombs dropped right along the A259. Capt Allnett's house near the bridge was destroyed.

Taken about 1925. On the left is part of the Berkshire Block of dormitories and the steps and staging for the children to make their way across the main road to the beach. A few buildings in Jefferstone Lane are visible. The white house, which was ex-Royal Flying Corps, is now Sunshine and Showers playschool. On the extreme right is the canteen, later the Camp tuckshop.

A later photograph showing children and teachers taking part in school sports. Buildings of the Yorkshire complex are in the background.

The Four Winds Cafe was a wooden structure built immediately in front of the Sands Hotel (presumably without planning permission). It was very close to the seashore and owned by a Mrs Negus. To the left another ex-army hut. They seemed very popular around this area. This was also a cafe known as The Seaview. It belonged to Mr Taylor who owned a considerable amount of land and building plots on the New Romney side of the New Cut. He was a builder and developer who constructed several bungalows along the main road and the lane that bears his name. All the bungalows were built of two skins of concrete blocks – try fixing a picture to the wall! The chimneybreasts were constructed from shuttered concrete – try knocking one down! The Seaview Café stood where the Gazedown Estate is today.

NDS HOTEL, ST. MARY'S BAY.

The Sands Hotel, built on what was known as the 'Outlands' which belonged originally to Jesson Farm. Some parts of this area would be under water when the sea seeped beneath the sea wall. I remember the wonderful times we had as boys when it was frozen over, especially in the winter of 1947. Built on the high ground and near the seashore in the early 1920s the three 80 foot long army huts were purchased, surplus to the War Department from Sandling Camp and erected to form an open square. One hut was divided into eight double rooms, the second into sixteen single rooms. The third housed the kitchen, dining room, lounge and bar. A wide veranda ran around the three huts on the sea side. The hotel was owned at one time by Frank Finn who sold it to some business people from London. Subsequently Mr Finn, who had extended some of the buildings prior to the sale started a building firm with his brother. Thus the firm F & R Finn was born. Later they developed a lot of St Mary's Bay and became a significant employer in the village. During the Second World War the hotel received a direct hit from a bomb. A boilerman and several soldiers who were billeted there were killed. Repaired after the war the Sands continued as a hotel and was very busy in the 40s and 50s. It was later pulled down and replaced by the Sands Motel. The bulldozer later removed that and now the land is awaiting redevelopment.

A very good view after the road widening in the 1950s. On the far left is the brick wall of the new bridge over the cut. Major Herbert's house is visible amongst the trees on the opposite side of the road. Following the road up are the Berkshire Block, the camp tuck shop and the old transport garages housing the St Mary's Bay Stores and Post Office.

This photograph was taken in the 1920s before Major Herbert's house was built. Motorised traffic was very sparse in those days but children can be seen gathering to make a safe crossing to the beach.

The same scene in the late 30s shows how narrow the main road was, especially the bridge where two lorries would have a job passing each other. The young man in the foreground is wearing plus fours, typical of the period and the girl is in camp uniform. Perhaps the girl on the other side of the road is her friend, patiently waiting while she is chatted up! In the 1940s a pill-box was constructed close to the spot where the couple are standing. Built into a bank it was manned by soldiers and a sentry would stop everyone and ask for their identity cards.

The Duke of York with the Camp Commandant, Captain J.O. Patterson returning from the beach after a swim. The photo shows them coming off the main road and walking down Jesson Lane. The Duke was a regular visitor to the camp in the 1920s.

A large group of boys, mostly from public schools, photographed near one of the dormitories on the camp. The Duke, wearing a sports jacket is in the second row, fifth from the right.

Games were played and competitions held. The boys in the picture are competing over some kind of assault course. All were encouraged to take part in such 'character-building' activities.

Two more views of some of the activities on the Camp during the Duke of York's era.

The York Hall was the main dining hall of the camp. Here the tables are set up for breakfast in real military style. More than two hundred children would sit down at one session. I remember as a boy just after the war going to concerts and parties in this building at Christmas. These events were organised by the church. This hall was one of the last places used for turkey plucking before the camp was pulled down.

This photo taken in the 20s, shows another view of the Berkshire Block from the main road at the New Romney end. All the buildings in this complex were given the names of towns in the county of Berkshire. From left to right are the Wantage and Ascot dormitories, teachers' quarters and the Early Hall. The buildings look like what they were – ordinary army huts – but they were brick built and looked quite smart when painted and tidied.

The Holiday Camp looking towards Dymchurch with boys playing cricket on the very large sports ground. The dormitories directly behind them are the Berkshire Block. The buildings to the left which are in Jefferstone Lane are now the playschool.

The Lancashire Block taken down by the railway showing from left to right Burnley, Birkenhead and Birkdale dormitories and Barrow Hall. In front are the army style ablutions, which were very basic in the early years of the camp. Other names come to mind from this area – Blackburn, Liverpool and Accrington. When I was a young boy I would associate them with football teams as I listened to the results on the wireless. Unfortunately some of these clubs are now out of the football league.

This early picture of the camp was taken from the bridge over the New Cut looking towards Dymchurch. The rock wind-breaks are now part of the garden of the house which stands on the site. Both Captain Allnett and Major Herbert made their homes here.

The camp hospital was built opposite the coal yard in Jesson Lane and staffed by full time nurses with the local doctors on call. During the holiday season it would be quite busy with children being taken in with minor injuries and illnesses. The original Royal Flying Corps hospital was just up the lane from this building and was bought from the War Department by Lt Chapman

The playing field and some of the new dormitories – Ripon, Leeds and Huddersfield – built after the war. Behind them to the left is the new tall chimney of the camp kitchen and the roofs of the Jesson Lane block of shops. At about this time the highlight of the summer for us local boys was the arrival of the French girls who came over from Lille for their summer holiday.

This photograph must have been one of the last taken of the Holiday Camp whilst it was still operating. The entrance is where the children lined up to be escorted across the road to the path that led to the seashore. The traffic was much lighter in those days. The striped porch in the picture was the entrance to the main office.

A train crossing the Duke of York's bridge over the New Cut at St Mary's Bay. Designed by Henry Greenly & Son the 55-foot girder bridge was a replica of one span of the Canadian National Railway's famous 25 span bridge across the St Lawrence river in Montreal. The bridge was constructed in steel but became unsafe and in 1968 was replaced by a standard bridge.

St Mary's Bay station. The large building behind the train was the camp power station. Here two large paraffin engines generated all the electricity for the camp lighting, and the pump for the main drainage which ran out raw into the sea near the New Cut outfall.

Originally known as Jesson Camp Station, now St Mary's Bay Station. Behind the first two carriages of the train is one of Captain Tucker's bungalows originally used as laboratories and dark room by the Royal Flying Corps. The big barn on the right, which stood in what is now Nesbit Road was the cowshed and dairy. After the cows were milked they would walk down the road and cross the railway at the end of the platform to graze on the old airfield. At the Jesson Lane end of the barn was a small shop where home made ice cream was sold in the days when the farm belonged to Mr Whitehead.

Looking towards Dymchurch near the sluice of the New Cut. This was known as a danger spot when we were young. If you were swimming near the sluice when the tide was going out and the gates were open the surge of water could sweep you out to sea. In those days a lot of the holiday camp children would play there and several had to be rescued. My father whilst working on the sea wall managed to save one small boy by pulling him out by one arm. Over the air shaft (the big block sticking out to sea) is a large sign with the word DANGER printed on it.

JESSON LANE, ST. MARY'S BAY.

Jesson Lane. The block of shops was built in the early 1950s by the local builders F&R Finn. In this picture is Mrs Funnell's drapery shop. The cafe and restaurant were owned by Mr Ambrose. The other shop, which is around the corner, was a greengrocer and later became E & N Paine's general store. The owner was a local man affectionately known as 'Cobby'. He remained there until he retired and the shop is now the Post Office owned by Brian Edwards and his wife. The dark building next door to the shops was Teelin Bungalow where the May family lived for many years. It was this bungalow that gave the Teelin Estate its name. Behind the bungalow is the Bailiff's Sergeant, formerly Mr Hopkins' General Store and Off Licence. The shop was divided into two with beers, wines and spirits on one side and groceries on the other. In the right hand window was a large, grey, model elephant advertising Fremlins, 'Kent's Best Beer'. The elephant was operated by electricity. Its trunk would move up and down, its ears backwards and forwards and the tail would wag. It used to fascinate me every time I passed the shop on my way to and from school. The main building became the Bailiff's Sergeant when the off-licence closed and a new general store was built in the early 50s.

A later picture of the shops in Jefferstone Lane taken in the 70s. Teelin Bungalow has gone and in its place, next door to Mrs Knott's drapery shop is Jeff Reddecliff's Hardware Shop. The Palm Grove restaurant was owned by Colin Sales, and Dick and Scottie were in the Bailiff's Sergeant. By now a proper path had been constructed on the left-hand side of the lane.

The Corner Shop (camp tuck shop) taken in the late 50s or early 60s. The main kitchens and the York Hall complex are behind the two poles. The white building on the extreme right is the Jubilee Hall built in 1935, the year of King George V's Silver Jubilee. It was used as the village hall until the new one was built.

A young Dave Wood outside the Bailiff's Sergeant General Store in the late 1950s. The inn sign was taken from a portrait of the then Bailiff's Sergeant, Bill Cook. The first landlord was Bob Hollis and his partner Mrs Booth. My old chap and his mate Scary Austin and some of the other customers nicknamed the pub 'The Rat and Cat'.

Outside Marshlands Bakery, 1951. Barbara Henley; Joan Whitehead; Jean Coombs; Jessie Kirkland in the background; apprentice baker Ray Crook sitting.

All Saints Church. Captain Allnett gave the land to St Mary's Bay so that a church could be built. The captain had been impressed by the drawing skills of one of the young draughtsman at his office in Manchester and asked him to design a church along simple and practical lines. Up until this time, Sunday services had been held in the local coal shed. Before services could begin it had to be cleaned out and the tools put away. In 1938, the Bishop of Dover laid the foundation stone in the presence of the Rt Rev Alfred Rose, the High Sheriff of Kent and Major Teichman Dervill. Following the new pastoral reorganisation scheme in 1983, the church became the Parish Church of St Mary's Bay. A vicarage was built and its first resident was the Rev. Mark Roberts.

William Body, a founder member of All Saints' Church and for many years a Churchwarden. I remember him ringing the bell before the Sunday morning service.

Golden Sands Holiday Camp. Built before the war and used by the army during that period. During the summer of 1944 the USA Army had a battery of anti-aircraft guns in the field beyond the chalets. These were used to fire at the incoming Doodlebugs. Later, in its heyday the camp was known as the Golden Sands Country Club and was owned by the Maddieson family who also had camps at Greatstone and Camber. Many holidaymakers who came down liked the area so much they returned every year. Some even moved down and bought property locally. The former world snooker champion Steve Davis used to come down for his holiday when he was a young lad.

Another view of the camp showing some of the chalets and the well-kept gardens.

Dunstall Lane in the late 1940s. When he took this view the photgrapher would have been standing in front of the site of Martello Tower No 26. On the left is Dunstall House. Built before the war of asbestos and wood, the chalet-style bungalow was refurbished in 1950 by V Apps & Son. Obscured by reeds to the right of the lane is the 'Old Gobsden Sewer' (now Cobsden), which in 1800 flowed under the road and out to sea. The sewer was diverted and now runs alongside the A259 to Dymchurch. Towards the rear of the photo in the field on the right are two of the flat-roofed bungalows built in the late 30s and similar in design to those on The Links Estate. If the war had not started in 1939 many more dwellings of this kind would have been built on this field which is now the site of The Fairway. A building programme had begun in 1938 and a few bungalows, including a show house, were built.

The Dymchurch end of St Mary's Bay taken in the 1930s. The white building left of centre is the Cobsden Cafe. In those days St Mary's Bay had a number of tearooms. There was another one near here in Spring Hollow. It was owned by Mrs Righten who gave it the name Mar.Jac.Ed after her children. The site of Martello Tower No 27 was on the right-hand side of the picture. I shall always remember the telegraph poles because the wind used to make the wires whistle. During the war when we went to school there would sometimes be loads of silver foil strips hanging from them. This was a radar-jamming device known as a 'window'.

Cobsden Bungalow built by William Body of Tenterden in 1900. Flat-roofed and constructed of concrete. The shingle and sand for the mix were wheel-barrowed from the shore. Later another storey was added and it became Cobsden Cafe. Then another shop was built on the side. The Café is now known as the 'Chippy'.

This photograph taken at the entrance to the estate shows the flags flown to attract customers to view the show house, which was floodlit at night. These bungalows sold very quickly just before the war.

Links Crescent as the estate was originally known, built in the late 30s. These were cheap flat-roofed holiday bungalows. Although built of breezeblocks, when plastered and painted white they looked quite attractive, especially with their stained-glass French doors. Rabson & Son, the New Romney butchers are delivering on the estate .

A Local Tragedy

One of my most vivid memories of the Links Estate concerns an horrific double murder and suicide which occurred there on 21st January 1947.

Some time during November of the previous year locals became aware of a new family living on the estate. There was a middle-aged man with a much younger woman and a girl of about twelve. Very little was seen of the woman. The man, Fred Russell did most of the shopping and often called at the Post Office Stores where my mother sometimes worked. Among the provisions he bought was tinned meat and vegetables issued during the war by the Ministry of Food and widely known as MV. Some said the meat came from whales. I hated the stuff. Anyway, Mr Russell was given the nickname 'Old MV'.

The woman with whom Russell was living was not his wife. In fact, her name was Elizabeth Wigley. She was separated from her husband and the young girl was her daughter.

On the afternoon of 21st January Elizabeth Wigley answered a knock at the door to find her husband David standing on the step. He told her he was looking for Russell. At the time Russell was working in Jesson Lane. On his return he was confronted by Wigley who was armed with a German automatic pistol. After a brief exchange of words Wigley shot Russell four times. Mrs Wigley attempted to escape through the back door and was gunned down on the garden lawn. After sending his daughter to fetch the police Wigley turned the gun on himself.

Some time after this tragic event the Dymchurch Morturary attendant was having a drink in the Ocean Pub when he overheard some customers arguing about Wigley's size.

"He was the same size as me", the attendant said, "I'm wearing his suit."

The Rugby Club's Camp

Rugby Camp St. Mary's Bay. 6,

In 1899 two old Rugbeians bought some land near the seashore with the outbuildings which had been part of the old Coastguard Station. The new buildings they erected became a permanent camp where boys, and later girls from the Notting Gate and Notting Hill areas of London could come down for a holiday by the sea. In 1903 William Temple also an old Rugbeian and later Archbishop of Canterbury, stayed there. The caretaker's house was built in 1922 in memory of the 117 gallant members of the Notting Hill Rugby Clubs who were killed in the 1914-18 war. The property belongs to Rugby School, founded in 1567 by Lawrence Sheriff and immortalised in *Tom Brown's Schooldays*. Famous headmasters have included Matthew Arnold, and two who later became Archbishops of Canterbury, Drs Tate and Temple. The school motto is "By praying and by working".

RUGBY MISSION, ST. MARY'S BAY.

Looking towards Dymchurch, another view of the Rugby Club's Camp or 'Mission' as it was known. In the distance on the left is the Sea View Café.

Opposite: *Three photos of the Sea View Café, the first one taken from the main A259 Road. The Sea View was a converted army hut. A tearoom was added by Mr Taylor in the twenties. After the War the owners were Mr and Mrs Smithson who also had the contract to supply the refreshments for the dances held in the drill hall during the late 40s and 50s. Two of the last proprietors were Mr and Mrs Inchcombe. Mrs Inchcombe was a dressmaker by profession and in 1960 she made my wife's wedding dress. Soon after the Inchcombes retired the building was demolished and replaced by the Gazedown Estate. The second picture was taken from the bank of the New Cut looking towards New Romney and the third shows tents and campers in the garden during the 1930s.*

People & Local Events

St Mary's Bay Garage in the 1930s. The business was started by Mr A Cusack and later taken over by Crouch's of Ashford. It is amazing how many brands of petrol and oil were available then – BP, Power, Redline, National, Benzol and Pratts. The large car parked on the forecourt was used as the local taxi. If you look down the same road today most of the bungalows are the same. Over on the Rugby Club and to the extreme right the little black hut that belonged to Mr Coker, the fisherman from Dymchurch is just visible.

Ian (Dick) Dewey painting the garage in 1957. Petrol is priced at 4s 3d and Derv a halfpenny more – just over 21 pence in today's money. Dick worked as a builder and decorator and still lives in St Mary's Bay.

Pirates Spring, known locally as the Blind School was a Sunshine Home for blind babies. It was built in 1937 by the contractors Geo.Walker and Slater & Co and was up and running for a year or so before the dark clouds of war gathered and it had to be closed. It was taken over by the Royal Navy and used as an observation post. After the war it was returned to the National Institute for the Blind and finally closed in 1960.

The last Christmas party at the school showing the staff with some of the children. Back row, left to right: Miss Hiner (Matron), Edna, Margaret, Jean, Marion, Mrs Smith, Valerie, Maureen, Mrs Wood.

Middle row: Hillary, Mr Pitt (Father Christmas), Barbara, Miss Pitt (Cook), Mrs Heasman. Front row: Jill, Mavis, Miss Ellard (Teacher) with Bing, the dog

Taylor's Lane. This photo was taken when the road was nothing more than a beach track. The white building on the right was then the first dwelling in the lane. It was called Sun Dial and was later the home of the Pierce family. Mr Pierce was blind and a trained basket maker. He used to make us shrimp baskets which were first class.

A pre-war picture of the A259 Road at what is now the entrance to Taylors Lane. In about 1950 Romney Marsh District Council decided to build the Newlands Estate. A new road and footpaths were constructed taking some of the garden of Marigolds, the bungalow on the right which was owned by Major and Mrs Wyatt. Mrs Wyatt used to play the piano at the village concerts The house nearest the camera was the home of Miss Hobbs and her sister. Their brother, Dr Hobbs lived in The Sands next door.

The Bay Singers performing in St Mary's Bay Church Hall in the early 1970s. They also sang at other venues around the area. The group was led by Mrs Launchbury and included Mrs Wyatt, Mrs Dawson, Yvonne Finn, Edna Haisell, Chris Wallace, Tom Hussey, Dave Thorpe, Barbara Hussey, Rene Dimmock and some young village boys and girls.

The Arlynton Players who performed concerts on Wednesday evenings in the Church Hall.

Left to right: Jean Coombs; Bevan Lorrimer; Florie Hunt (sitting); Percy Hunt; Shirley Heron (sitting); Tony Walters; Arthur Parker; Lyn Walters.

St Mary's Bay Branch of the Royal British Legion dinner held in the top room of the Levin Club in 1950(?) I am able to identify only a few of the guests.

Standing, left to right: Mrs Blyton; Mrs Rodman; Miss Bourne; Mr Rodman; Bill Ball; Mr Harradine.

'Cobby' Paine is sitting on the left nearest the camera. Harry Hogben is nearest the camera on the right and to his right at the same table are Ted Stafford and Arthur Foord.

Most of us boys who lived down the lane would play football and cricket in our school holidays. The pitch was any field that had not been ploughed up by the farmer. We moved from field to field and in the end stayed in one at the bottom of Jesson Lane, which was eventually taken over by the local council and turned into a Sports Ground. Jesson Cricket Club was formed, a square was prepared for the wicket and a pavilion built. The Club's headquarters was at the Levin Club. A football club followed soon after.

Jesson Cricket Team in the early 50s

Back row from the left: Dennis (Ratter) Beale, Dick Apps, Sonny Woollard, Jack Burden, Roy Britton, Cyril Jenner. Front row from left: Billy Finn, Jeff Best, Albert Jenner, William (Bill) Ball, Robin Apps, Bernard Jenner.

Jesson Football Team

Back row from left: Ted Sagger; Eric Finn; Ernie Woolard; Mick Owens; Fred White; George Binnon; Lewis Beale; Peter Royce. Front row from the left: Jack Wall; Not known; Dick Apps; Fred Coates; Jim Chivers; D. Knight

The Levin Club children's party at the Drill Hall St Mary's Bay in 1950 or 1951. Shown in the photograph are Mrs Crisp; Joyce Fagg; June Beale; Thelma Jenner; Harry Hogben; Mr Lodman; Nancy Link; Mrs Hathaway; Shirley Heron; Roy Hathaway; Jim Breeze; Roy Evershed; Peter Colmer; Mrs Hogben; Marge Coveney; Gwen Britton; Milly Bennett; Tony Paine; George Hogben; Dolly Dickinson; Mrs Colmer; Mrs Bracken and a number of unidentified individuals.

The parade of the 507 Company RASC Territorial Army complete with their lorries.

Back row: H Rose; A Edmonds; N Hulkes; W Edwards; D Smith; D Crooks; D Riddles; L.Fisher; F Johns; D Harridine; Not known; F Ledger; R Britton; A Wood; A Portage; C Manning; Not known; Not known; D McCarty; S Pellet; L Vincent; Not known; Not known; ? Drinkwater.

Front row: J Stewart; K Horton; B Stewart; H Cromack; S Flaxton; Not known; Lt Boag; F Murphy. The names of the remaining five men are not known.

This photograph, taken in the early 50s shows Captain J C Allnett and his daughter Peggy presenting the Freedom of St Mary's Bay to Lt Boag of the 507 Company RASC Territorials

In the mid 1930s Captain J C Allnett was able to persuade the War Office to allow him to start a territorial unit at St Mary's Bay holiday camp. In 1936 the Romney Marsh detachment of the Dover Cinque Ports Searchlight Company, Royal Engineers was born, and known as Allnett's Terriers. To warrant a drill hall the unit needed to muster one hundred recruits, officers and NCOs being provided. The number was achieved in 1938 and a hall was duly provided. During the war dances were held there, especially during 1944 when we were invaded by the Yanks. They livened up the place and the lorries ferried in girls from all over the Marsh. Us kids used to stand by the door and watch what was going on inside – and outside!

St Mary's Bay Cadets RASC photographed at the Drill Hall in the late 50s

Back Row: D Dixon; G Wood; J Best; R Beale; I. Booth; M Hunt; Not known; J Deeley.

Middle Row: R Apps; M Loader; Not known; Not known; WO1 Anderson; Not known; T Paine.

Front Row: F Harridine; P Hedges; I Brody; D Weller; E Booth.

The Royal Berkshire Regiment was stationed at St Mary's Bay and their dance band played at the old Jesson Club. Double bass player Philip Bishop married local girl Cicely Coombs in 1945.

The 'Old Contemptibles' at the Drill Hall in the mid 50s with some of the T.A boys.
Back row, left to right: Derek Harridine; Not known; Not known; Ernie (Bones) Williams; Peter Kennedy (with bagpipes); George (Bunny) Beale; Sid (Dugger) Crooks; John Beale; Mr Thompson; Wally Edwards; Sid Flaxton; Barty Stewart; Norman (Will) Williams.
Sitting: George Fuller (Mr Mipps, church gardener and Dymchurch grave digger); Henry Upton; 'Bantam' Beeching; Walter (Bunkle) Roots; Frank (Flipper) Woodland; Les (Weasel) Haisell. Crouching: Joey Stewart. Photograph G & F Daws

By now it looks as if the beer has begun to work!

Left to right: 'Bunkle' Roots; John Beale; Les Haisell; Josie Edwards; Bantam Beeching; Joey Stewart; Henry Upton; Peter Kennedy; Barty Stewart; Derek Harridine. Photograph G & F Daws.

Outside the old Jesson Club

Back row, left to right: Ted Downs (Steward); Jim Breeze; George Bartlett; Hugh Owens; Cyril Jenner (coal merchant); Ben Flisher (St Mary's Bay Post Office); Wally Mullet.

Front row, left to right: Ralph Taylor; Tom Dickenson; Bill Gudgeon. The identity of the young boy is not known.

Most of the men in the above photograph came to St Mary's Bay during the war. The club was another former Flying Corps building, situated in Jesson Lane on the right near Jesson Farm. It opened in 1922 and one of the founder members was T T Tucker, husband of E Nesbitt author of *The Railway Children*. After Tucker's death in 1936 a plaque bearing his name was mounted on the chimneybreast in the small bar.

The club consisted of a large bar, private bar, snooker room with a full size table and beyond that a dance hall with catering facilities. At the very end was a private dwelling owned by Miss Kate Paget who used part for a greengrocer's shop. Just before the war I think there was a split between the committee and some members who wanted another club. F&R Finn built the Levin, which was always referred to as the 'New Club'.

During the war it was used as a NAAFI and was at one time run by 'Cobby' Paine. The old club carried on after the war and was later sold to Ted Brews and Jim who renamed it Pope's Club after Pope's Hotel at Littlestone, their previous venture. Eventually it became the Night Rider (or Hut 29 after the Army Game) until it partly burnt down, later to be demolished. The site has since been developed.

The Levin Dart Team 1951, winners of the Folkestone Herald Cup and the Harry Merritt Cup. Harry Merritt was once landlord of The Ship, New Romney

Back row from the left: Sam Hills; Albert Best; George Dearlove; Les Bessel; Cyril Jenner; Eric Finn; Bill Gudgeon.

Middle Row: Jock Singer; Bill Finn; Ted Downs; Ted Best.

Front row: Billy Finn; Percy Best; Not known; Arthur Simmons owner of the Levin Club).

The Lost Fishing Fleets of Dymchurch and Littlestone

Dymchurch

In the 1800s each little village and hamlet around the coast had its own fishing fleet and the Dymchurch boats worked from the beach at the end of the sea wall near High Knock. In those days the sea wall was constructed with faggots of hawthorn and blackthorn, mixed with clay. Although this method of construction provided an effective defence against the sea and continued to be used well into the nineteenth century, modern methods were eventually adopted.

Highknock Bridge Dymchurch, built over the Cobsden sewer. This photo was taken about 1903. The Dymchurch fishing boats would have been pulled up on the beach at the end of the sea wall opposite the bridge.

The Dymchurch Sea Wall, looking towards Hythe. I have included this photo because years ago holes like this were common and most of the repairs had to be carried out using hand tools only. That being said, my father who is in the centre of the picture, and his mate, are operating a primitive jackhammer. A large can of petrol is standing on a rock near them. Rocks were moved by large crowbars. At the base of the hole clay would be distributed, rocks dropped in at random and wedged as a temporary measure until the weather improved. Then the rocks would be set in properly and pointed up with cement. This work was known as 'tide work' because the men started later each day as the tide receded. I remember an occasion in the 1950s when large bays of concrete near the Sands Hotel, were lifted up like sheets of hardboard by the seas. When we suffered a severe gale of wind from the north, the damage was caused by the ground swell. As the waves turned over, they trapped massive volumes of air. The air, unable to escape was compressed by the weight of water and eventually exploded causing the damage.

Dymchurch about 1900. My father was born that year in The Dormers – the little white cottages in the centre of the photo. In those days they were fishermen's homes and later became tearooms and a restaurant. In the next block of cottages to the right the artist Paul Nash stayed while he was in Dymchurch. He painted several seascapes including the Dymchurch sea wall.

Around the turn of the century, with rumours of the proposed construction of a concrete wall, the fishermen decided to move their boats to the stretch of beach near the site of the old St Mary's Coastguard near the Rugby Camp.

After many years' work the new wall, built under the auspices of the Romney Marsh Level was completed in 1927.

My grandfather Frank Haisell (nicknamed Weasel) was the skipper of a small boat called the *Little Wanderer FE150*, owned by his Aunt Ann Young from Dymchurch. In 1902 Mrs Young decided to purchase a new and bigger vessel, the *Grace Darling* (no connection with the lighthouse heroine of the same name). The boat was built in Hastings and my grandfather sailed her home on her maiden voyage. She was named after his daughter Grace, my aunt who was born in 1902.

My father Les with his sister Grace after whom the Grace Darling was named.

Although by today's standard the boat was small she was the largest in the fleet at 23 feet with a beam of 9 feet. With a gross weight of 5.12 tons she was divided into three sections by two bulkheads.

The front section was a closed compartment with access through a hatch on top. This was known as the forepeak. There was just enough room for some of the crew to get in and shelter from the elements. There was also an oil stove that would be lit to make tea or to cook.

It is difficult to imagine being down there with all those fumes, trying to balance a kettle of scalding water with the boat rolling about on the sea. With so much wood around, coated with linseed oil and tar it is a wonder they never set the boat alight.

The middle section of the boat was the net room where the deep cotton drift nets were stowed. These nets, fitted with bunches of cork floats or 'bobbers' were set across the tide and hung in the sea like a long curtain into which the fish would swim. To mark the ends of the net furthest from the boat, there would be a large cork with a pole and flag attached called a 'dahn'. At night a lantern would be added and during the herring season, the bay would be a mass of twinkling dahn lights stretching from Hythe to Dungeness. Today, there are very few drifters left.

The rear of the boat was known as the stern sheets. From here she was steered by a tiller. A large lantern was fixed to the mizzenmast.

The bulkhead between the net room and the stern sheets housed a pump that was one of the most important items of equipment on board. It was of simple design in the form of a square-shaped housing made from four pieces of wood. A plunger attached to a leather valve was inserted into the housing and the pump was primed with a bucket of water. When the nets were being hauled aboard the cotton from which they were made held considerable volumes of water and the pump was in constant use on the way home.

A very heavy and wide boat the *Grace Darling* had a crew of three men and one boy. In 1915 there were two boys and I wonder if that had anything to do with the Great War and the shortage of manpower. Today this type of vessel would be worked with a crew of two but when she was built there were no engines and the boat had to be sailed and rowed.

When my father was a young boy he went for a trip catching herrings with his dad and the rest of the crew. He was so cold they put him down below. The fumes from the paraffin oil stove combined with the rolling of the boat, made him so sick it put him off for life. He never went to sea again.

Another vessel was the *Daisy*. She was slightly smaller than the *Gracie* and owned by a very good Dymchurch fisherman, Jonney Tolhurst. I believe Jim Coker's father, another Dymchurch man started fishing in this boat. Albert Flisher was a member of this crew. The boat registration number was FE 90 which resulted in Mr Flisher being given the nickname 'Ninety', a name he retained for the rest of his long life.

Another of life's characters was an oriental man who lived in a shed on the beach. According to local belief he was not very fond of soap and water and acquired the name 'Chinaman Darkee'. He did all the odd jobs and helped to get the boats afloat. When the boats came ashore he would help members of the crew operate the capstan to drag them from the water. At night he would light the paraffin lamp to guide the boats back to the bleak and desolate beach.

Other boats fishing from Jesson around this time were the *Gratitude FE23*, owned and skippered by Jim Peggy Flisher; *Boney Bess FE100* skippered by R. Pope; Fred Smith's *Foam FE205* and the *Invicta FE194* owned by Alf Henley. He and Mr Smith had kettle net stands down on the sands during the season. The boats' mode of fishing was mainly drifting for sprats, mackerel and herring in their respective seasons.

The herring season was the most important and a good one provided money to see the fishermen through the leaner times. During the First World War my mother worked at the City of London public house in Dymchurch. On still mornings she told me she would hear the clip clop of the horses and the sound of the steel rimmed cartwheels as they made their way through the streets of Dymchurch to collect the fish landed at Jesson. Sometimes when they returned later in the day, the carts would be loaded to the brim. The fish were taken to Hythe and sold fresh or cured as kippers or bloaters. Some were put on the train at Sandling for London. The main carriers were Cloke's and Brenchleys. There were several herring hangs in Dymchurch at that time and a lot of fish were cured locally. Some of the older generation recall walking home on frosty nights and smelling the wonderful aroma of the oak sawdust burning as the herring were being cured. Today it is very hard to market herrings. I do not know why this should be the case as they are full of protein and natural oil and so versatile. I expect it is the bones or the fact that they don't come neatly prepacked in a square box.

Grandfather packed up fishing and became the licensee of the Warren Inn at New Romney. Later he moved back to Dymchurch and spent as much time as he could shrimping and setting lines for the fish on the sands. He also would breed (make) his own shrimp nets, a skill he had learned as a boy being brought up in a fishing family. In the winter he sat by the fire in the kitchen with his work hooked up on a nail fixed in the side of the chimney breast and breed the meshes with a net needle. This was a very tedious job because of the small size of the shrimp net mesh. He worked all winter making and rigging the nets to different sizes including small ones for children. They would be taken up to Henry Upton's shop and sold to holidaymakers.

The *Grace Darling* carried on fishing and a 12hp Kelvin engine was fitted. It must have been like heaven after all those old sailing and rowing days. On one occasion in 1922 when the boat was skippered by her owner Ernie (Brigham) Young with Andy Austin as crew, they had a very large catch of herring estimated at over two last, (a last was 10,000 fish). When they managed to get to shore and the boat touched the sand she broke her back through the weight of the fish. This would have been about 600 stone plus the weight of the wet nets and the water in the boat. Later she was pulled up and laid at Jesson for some time, never to go to sea again.

In those days herring were always counted as they were boxed up. After being shaken out of the nets they were picked off the beach. Because the fish are particularly slippery it is difficult to pick up more than two when sorting them. Thus a count of four, known as a warp came about. Thirty-three warp made a long hundred a traditional measure of one hundred and thirty two fish. To the wholesaler the extra thirty-two fish were to compensate for those that had lost their heads when they were removed from the nets. Such fish would be useless for bloating because the sticks on which they were hung in the smokehouse were passed through their heads.

Most of the fishermen in those days were regular church- or chapelgoers. My grandfather was no exception. On Sundays he would never go to sea before midnight and the kettle nets blythes were left open so the fish could swim away. Sunday fish were known as the devil's fish.

The concrete sea wall built by the Romney Marsh Level in 1927 was later extended to Littlestone. Part of the labour force was drawn from the depressed South Wales mining areas. To mark completion and to proclaim its magnificence the local dignitaries had a plaque, complete with all their names mounted on the wall. But in just three years the sea wall was in ruins having been breached in several places. A replacement was built by, I believe, J. B. Edwards. My father and Freddie Combes from Hythe had the job of removing the plaque with jackhammers. This was done to save a lot of red faces. With the coming of the sea wall the fishing fleet had dwindled to a couple of boats

Mr E Coker was asked to leave and was offered a sum of money as an incentive to do so. When he reported the situation to the local fishery officer he was told to stay. Eventually the Kent River Authority provided him with a proper ramp and a hardstanding on which to keep his boat. In 1961 Jim Coker kindly allowed me to use the site and hut and I was the last fisherman to operate a registered fishing boat from that beach. By 1963 the sea had eroded the beach to such an extent that the River Board called in contractors to build a new toe at the bottom of the sea wall. It became impossible for me to launch my boat and I moved to Littlestone.

The ill-fated sea wall in 1935. The photograph shows Mr G Dewey with his son Ian (known as Dick) and their dog Patsy.

The Dymchurch fishing fleet photographed in 1903. The large boat in the foreground is the Grace Darling FE 96. *Other boats are the* Daisy *owned by Jonney Tolhurst, the* Invicta *belonging to Alf Henley. I cannot find any information about the white boat.*

Almost one hundred years later but on the beach at Littlestone rather than Dymchurch. The boats have changed very little since grandfather's day.

This photo was included to show kettle net poles, which are just visible between the groynes (breakwaters). The poles would run from the top of the beach to beyond the low water mark. Attached to them top and bottom would be a net forming a wall known as the range. Fish meeting the net would instinctively turn towards the sea only to be caught in the kettle – a circle of poles with net fixed around the end of the range. The Dymchurch families of the Henleys, Flishers and Smiths were the main operators of this method of fishing. I can remember the last nets to be set on the sands at Dymchurch by the Henley brothers, the last licence holders.

Two boats at Jesson in the mid 1920s. The large vessel is the Grace Darling *which was demasted and retired from fishing in 1922. The small cottage behind the boat is the* Russian House. *The St Mary's Coastguard Station was near this site. On the sands are boys on holiday at the Rugby Camp.*

The author in 1961, standing beside the Welcome Home RX109. *This was the last boat to fish from the beach at the Rugby Camp. It was once owned by Len Prebble's father and fished for many years from the beach at Dengemarsh. In 1963 with the beach in such a state from erosion I had to move her to Littlestone.*

Littlestone

Back in the 1900s the fishing fleet at Littlestone had been similar to that at Jesson. The boats were pulled up the beach in front of the Dormey House on the Parade. Later they moved further south to where the beach huts are now on the edge of The Greens.

The fishermen also helped man the lifeboat although from 1912 when the last lifeboat, the *Harry Wright Russell* came into service until 1928 when the station closed, there were only three service calls. The last coxswain was a local fisherman Charles (Jammer) Sharp. In 1996 the RNLI opened a station at Littlestone with an inshore rescue boat that is fully operational today.

The last surviving member of the Littlestone lifeboat crew was Albert Barnes. A fisherman and shrimper, he owned several boats including *Wild Flower FE162* and *Mayflower FE132*. I remember him in his later years riding his tricycle around the town of New Romney

The Polehills were another of the old families. They had the Victorian bathing machines which were pushed into the sea with the bathers inside. They also owned fishing boats. Frank had a vessel called *Hand in Hand FE 155* and Stan fished in *Augustine FE43*. During the war he worked a boat out of Rye called the *Skylark FE31* owned by Elam Ellis a builder and New Romney councillor who later became Mayor of the Town.

After he retired Stan Polehill would come down to the beach at Littlestone and help me pull nets over. He loved it, especially in the herring season as he said it reminded him of the old days. When he had had enough he would toddle off home on his bike with a feed of fish. You miss those characters.

The best fisherman was probably Freddie Mogg known as Old Froggy. He had two boats crewed by local men Sam Hills and Jack Mills. These were the *Ivy FE24* and the *Lois FE12*. Both were destroyed in 1941 in a tragic accident which resulted in Freddie's death.

Freddie lived in New Romney and used to cycle down to the beach. During the war the seashore was mined and large coils of barbed wire formed a defensive wall on the landside. The Greens at Littlestone were also mined and fishermen and the army had a narrow right of way that zigzagged across the beach to the boats. Apparently, on the day of his death Freddie had overslept and was late. He had lines on the sand and was anxious to get the fish off the hooks as the tide had started to flow. Some people said he had been balancing a basket on his handlebars (I do not know if that is true as it seems more likely he would have carried the basket on his back) and that he was riding his bike along the path through the minefield instead of walking. In any event he it appears he lost his balance and fell on a mine. Some say it set more off. Whatever the case, poor Freddie was blown to pieces and his boats seriously damaged. It is said his bike landed on the roof of the Grand Hotel (later Popes) which stood on the corner of the Parade and the Avenue.

Fishermen supplemented their earnings by catching shrimps. The famous 'Romney Browns' were in abundance at certain times of the year and as many as thirty shrimpers – not all professionals I hasten to add – could be seen in the sea at low water.

The shrimps would be brought up the sand in pails, sacks and proper baskets. Taking them home and cooking them was the test of a good shrimper. My grandfather said everybody could catch shrimps but cooking them properly was a different matter. The art is knowing how much salt to put in the brine and when to take the shrimps out of the boiling water. If undercooked they are soft and pappy; overdone they are like straw and will not come out of their shells

Shrimps were boxed up and put on the train for Hastings or London at New Romney station. On Sunday lunch times in all of the pubs in Dymchurch, New Romney and Lydd shrimps would be sold. Each individual would have his own pitch.

Today it would be impossible to make a living from fishing at St Mary's Bay or Littlestone because of the lack of fish and shrimps and also the restrictions of the tides. The area was also ideal for drift nets but with the market for herring and sprats being so depressed it is impossible to make any money out of them today.

The fishing boat Lois FE12 built in Deal in 1912. This photo was taken before the Second World War. The vessel was one of those destroyed by a mine in 1941 when its owner/skipper, Freddie Moggs set it off on his way across the Greens to his boat.

A fine picture of Albert Barnes of New Romney mending nets. He is wearing a traditional blue gransly, serge trousers and cheesecutter hat, the dress of all fishermen from that era. Albert served for 35 years in the RNLI, 28 years as 2nd Coxswain of the Littlestone Lifeboat. He was the last serving member to die. Born in Lydd he started fishing as a boy and continued until he was 84 years old. He died in 1950 aged 88. When I was attending New Romney C.E. School, I remember him riding his tricycle around the town

Looking towards Dungeness about 1903, not a building to be seen, only the drinking fountain (still there today) and the sand dunes beyond. The boat in the foreground is The Dart FE129, *built in Hastings in 1897 and owned by Albert Bates. The bathing machines belonged to Mr Polehill and were used by residents and holidaymakers from the big houses on Littlestone front. You can see shrimp nets left out to dry – something you could not do today, as soon as you turned your back they would be gone! Also in view is the capstan which was used to pull the boats out of the water, a very hard and tedious job walking around and around holding on to a large pole.*

The Wild Flower FE162 *built at Rye in 1912, coming ashore under sail at Littlestone with Albert Barnes at the helm. Also on board are three ladies and a man who have probably been out on a trip around the Bay. Mr Barnes owned the boat between 1916 and 1924.*

The fishing beach at Littlestone photographed between the wars. Although the boats continued to carry sails, most now had engines fitted. The propeller on Freddie Moggs' boat the Lois is visible. By now boats were using beam trawls and the long pole of the beam is lying along the topside of Freddie's boat with net draped over it. The rest of the net is pulled out on the beach and the fishermen are 'cuffing' it over looking for holes to mend. Behind the boats are the big Victorian houses of Littlestone. Unfortunately, some have now been replaced by modern blocks of flats.

The seafront houses as they were in about 1900 with the Grand Hotel *(later* Popes*) behind the coast guard standing towards the left of the picture. The fishing boats were later moved further south to where the beach huts are today. In the foreground is local shrimper a young Albert Barnes. He must have a twelve-foot net, much bigger than the ones we use today, and no waders only thick serge trousers. My Gran told me when her father William Philpot (Billy Wiggles) came home from shrimping in the wintertime his beard and trousers would be as stiff as a board with frost. They would get him near the fire to thaw him out.*

This view shows the boats brought up in front of The Parade (Dormey House). The banks and hollows in front of the house indicate how the sea had receded over the years on this part of the coast. In the centre of the picture the water tower is standing on its own. The next building to the right is Mr Gladstone's home. The former Prime Minister used to come down for the sea air and to play golf. Beyond Mr Gladstone's house is Littlestone Life Boat House.

A very early postcard posted in 1904 showing the Grand Hotel (later Pope's) and other big houses on the Littlestone seafront. The fountain was erected to commemorate Queen Victoria's Diamond Jubilee.

The remains of the Jaarlen *as they appear today. Wrecked between Littlestone and St Mary's Bay, she washed ashore on 22nd October 1891, the same year the three coastguards from St Mary's Station perished while serving at the Littlestone lifeboat. The* Jaarlen *was a Norwegian barque loaded with timber, all pitchpine. Her cargo was sold locally, and an estate at Lydd is named after her.*

The Jaarlen *when she first came ashore.*

This photo was taken in the early 1900s. The boat in the foreground is the fishing lugger Mayflower FE132, *built in 1888 at Rye and owned by Albert Barnes. The boat was originally owned by the Griggs family and worked from Hythe.*

The Kingfisher *at Littlestone today. I could be the last to have a registered fishing boat at the above venue.*